$5·60

Bele buche e bele parleure

BELE BUCHE
E
BELE PARLEURE

A guide to the pronunciation of
medieval and Renaissance French
for singers and others

by
Jeannine Alton *and* Brian Jeffery

*Tecla Editions, Preachers' Court, Charterhouse,
London EC1M 6AS, England*

PRINTED IN SPAIN BY ARTES GRÁFICAS SOLER, S. A., JÁVEA, 28, VALENCIA (8)

I.S.B.N.: O 9502241 2 X (cloth)
I.S.B.N.: O 9502241 3 8 (paper)

DEPÓSITO LEGAL: V. 246 - 1977   I.S.B.N.: 84-399-6319-X

Music

PREFACE

*This book is intended for anyone who wishes to speak
or sing medieval or Renaissance French texts as authentical-
ly as possible. Singers will find it valuable when they wish
to sing such things as troubadour lyrics or the chansons of
Machaut or Dufay; so will actors, reciters, and students
of the language.*

*The information is given in three forms. First, the pro-
nunciation of French vowels and consonants from 1100 to
1600 is set out. Then the same information is arranged in
the form of a chart, so that for any given text, the state of
French pronunciation at that particular date may be seen
at a glance. Finally, twelve poems are presented which date
from between 1100 and 1600, with a commentary on their
pronunciation. To use this book, no knowledge of the history
of the French language is required, but familiarity with
present-day French is assumed.*

*A 35-minute cassette is available from the publisher on
which all the poems which appear in the book are spoken
in their original pronunciation. In addition, six of them are
sung on the cassette in musical settings of their own time:
one of them anonymous, and the others by Bernard de Ventadorn, Adam de la Hale, Machaut, Compère, and Lassus.*

*Though the work is not intended for the specialist, a
certain number of phonetic symbols must be recognized; they
are listed, with examples, on page 13.*

*No attempt of this kind can be more than an approxima-
tion. There is no incontrovertible evidence of historical
sounds, whether music or speech, such as recordings can
now provide. There is no reason to doubt that there were
many differences in pronunciation from one place (even one
village) to another, from one social class to another, and
from one period to another (perhaps very short periods), just*

7

as there are today. The boundaries between ecclesiastical and feudal estates; the lord's castle or court; the artisans' workshops in its shadow; the trade-guilds of the growing towns: all these could make divisions between men, their status and their means of communication. The great fairs; the trade-routes; pilgrimages and crusades; the temporal and spiritual weight of the Church; the slow extension of the royal power: these might unify and consolidate. The last of these — the monarchy with its lands in the Ile-de-France and its social, legal and administrative centre in Paris — is generally accepted as the linguistic standard for all hypothetical reconstructions such as this.

Because this book is specifically designed to help performers of works whose original authors and composers were almost invariably under the patronage of wealthy or educated persons, a somewhat conservative line has been drawn in the dating of many of the changes in pronunciation. This applies particularly to nasal vowels and final consonants, where we know that 'correct' and 'popular' versions co-existed for substantial periods of time. Preference has been given to the 'correct' alternative, but the 'popular' version has also been noted where its use may help to give to a song or poem a social as well as a local habitation.

Despite the recognition of Parisian or 'Francien' as a standard, other regions of France produced not only specific forms of speech but also a characteristic culture expressed in literature, often extending over many generations. The most important forms for the present purpose are Provençal, Picard, and Norman, and they are described on pages 24 to 29.

Finally, it should be noted that if a spelling is not listed in the first part of this book, or in the chart that follows, it should be pronounced as in modern educated Parisian French.

ACKNOWLEDGEMENTS

Our thanks are due to Dr. Nigel Wilkins and Dr. F. Sternfeld, and especially to Professor Roy Harris for generous help and advice; to Professor J. H. Marshall for his help with the section on Provençal; and to B. H. Blackwell and Cambridge University Press for permission to reproduce extracts from works published by them.

The performers on the cassette are:

Derek Coltman	*speaker*
Richard Apley	*countertenor*
Anthony Bremner	*countertenor*
Brian Burrows	*tenor*
Charles Corp	*tenor*
Anthony Ransome	*baritone*
June Baines	*tenor viol*
Michael Laird	*cornett*
Roger Brenner	*alto sackbut*
Peter Harvey	*bass sackbut*

Directed by Brian Jeffery

CONTENTS

PHONETIC NOTATION

The phonetic symbols used are those of the International Phonetic Alphabet. Square brackets are used for phonetic symbols; italics are used for spellings.

Vowels

[a]	*ami, femme*
[ɑ]	*pas, âge*
[e]	*été, j'ai*
[ɛ]	*mais, peine*
[i]	*cri, fine*
[o]	*chaud, eau, rose*
[ɔ]	*homme, donne*
[u]	*tout, vous, cour*
[y]	*tu, une*
[ø]	*feu, ceux*
[œ]	*jeune, sœur*
[ə]	*le, je*

[~] indicates a nasal vowel

Consonants

[b], [d], [f], [h], [k], [l], [m], [n], [p], [s], [t], [v], [w], [z] have their usual values.

[ʃ]	*chanter, chose*
[tʃ]	English *chant, church*
[ʒ]	*manger, jamais*
[dʒ]	English *Jack, June*
[ɲ]	*agneau, vigne*
[r]	Spanish *rojo*, Italian *tre*
[R]	*près, cœur, quatre*
[j]	*yeux, bien*
[ɥ]	*nuit, lui*
[λ]	Spanish *llamar*, Italian *figlio*
[θ]	English *thin*

Part 1

VOWELS AND CONSONANTS

VOWELS

(for nasal vowels, see pages 18 to 20)

A

(i) *a* is pronounced [a], as in modern French *arbre, cheval,* in all words until 1550; during the 16th century [ɑ] develops when [s] at the end of a word, or before another consonant, becomes silent; e.g., *pas, mât, âne, donnâtes.* Most of these words have a circumflex accent in modern French.

>   To 1550:   [a]
>   After 1550: [a], [ɑ]

(ii) *ai,* as in *faire, mais, raison,* is pronounced [ai] to about 1150, thereafter [ɛ]; in some verb-endings, such as *j'ai, j'aimai, j'aimerai,* the modern pronunciation [e] may be used from about 1250.

>   To 1150:   [ai]
>   1150-1250:   [ɛ]
>   After 1250: [ɛ], [e] in some verb-endings

(iii) *au,* as in *aube, autre,* is pronounced as the diphthong [au] to about 1300, then the diphthong [ao] to 1500, thereafter [o] as in modern French.

>   To 1300:   [au]
>   1300-1500:   [ao]
>   After 1500: [o]

E

(i) *ei*, as in early French *mei, curteis,* is pronounced [ei] to about 1150, [ɔi] to about 1200, then [uɛ]; for later stages see under **O** below (page 17).

(ii) Words spelt *eu*, as in *fleur, cheveux,* are pronounced [œ] from about 1150 to 1700. The modern French [ø] should not be used.

(iii) 'Feminine' or 'mute' *e* final or in monosyllables such as *je, ce,* is pronounced as in English *get* to about 1300, then more weakly [ə] like the second vowel in English *sofa* to about 1550, thereafter as in modern French.

> To 1300: as in English *get*
> 1300-1550: as in English *sofa*
> After 1550: as in modern French

The modern French [ø] should not be used before 1550.

(iv) 'Feminine' or 'mute' *e* before a vowel or diphthong, as in the old forms *mireoir, veu,* is pronounced [ə] to about 1300, thereafter silent.

(v) *eau*, as in *beau,* is pronounced [ɛau] to 1300, [ɛao] 1300-1500, [əo] to 1600. Modern French [o] is not accepted before the 17th century.

> To 1300: [ɛau]
> 1300-1500: [ɛao]
> 1500-1600: [əo]

I

Words spelt *ie*, as in *pied, fièvre,* are pronounced [ie] to about 1150, [je] to about 1400, thereafter as in modern French: [je] final, [jɛ] non-final.

> To 1150: [ie]
> 1150-1400: [je]
> After 1400: [je] final, [jɛ] non-final

Note that old forms such as *baisier, couchiez, mangié,* should be pronounced [je] to about 1400, thereafter [e].

O

(i)   The simple vowels [ɔ] as in *porte*, [u] as in *louer*, have not changed their pronunciation, though in the 16th century there was much variation between [ɔ] and [u] and many words changed their pronunciation and spelling. Early pre-16th century forms such as *souleil*, *fourme*, *coumencer*, should be pronounced [u].

(ii)   Words spelt *oeu*, as in *coeur*, *soeur*, like words spelt *eu* above, are pronounced [œ].

(iii)   *oi*, as in *voix*, *angoisse*, *gloire*, *joie*, is pronounced [oi] to about 1200, then [uɛ] (see also *ei* above). The pronunciation [wɛ] developed during the 13th century and remained the correct form until the 18th century. The pronunciation [wa] should not be used unless it is specifically intended to convey, from about 1300, the colloquial speech of the lower classes of Paris.

Note that verb-endings in *-ais* etc., adjectives of nationality such as *français*, *anglais*, words like *raide*, *frais*, *épais*, *connaître*, spelt with *ai*, should be pronounced [ɛ] from 1300.

> To 1200:   [oi]
> 1200-1300:   [uɛ], [wɛ]
> 1300-1600:   [wɛ], [ɛ] in cases noted above, [wa] in
>   colloquial Parisian.

U

(i)   *u*, as in *tu*, *vertu*, is pronounced [y].

(ii)   *ui*, as in *nuit*, *conduire*, is pronounced [yi] to about 1200, thereafter [ɥi] as in modern French.

> To 1200:   [yi]
> After 1200: [ɥi]

NASAL VOWELS

Nasalized articulation seems to have been very prevalent during the period covered by this guide. All vowels followed by [m], [n], or [ɲ] were nasalized at the approximate dates shown below.

The stages of this complicated phenomenon are not easy to chart precisely; there were variations between Parisian and provincial speech, as well as between what was deemed 'correct' and 'popular'. For reasons given in the preface, the information below aims at 'correct' Parisian speech; additional notes on 'popular' or provincial forms are given where relevant.

Note that the nasal consonant **as well as the vowel** continues to be pronounced until about 1500-1550, and that the vowel may change its value during the period of nasalization.

The process of de-nasalization, which determined the modern pronunciation of words like *femme, homme, aimer,* etc., was beginning in the 16th century. All vowels followed by a nasal consonant and another vowel thereafter gradually ceased to be pronounced with a nasal articulation. Thus, *bon* and *fin* remained nasalized, while *bonne* and *finir* lost their nasal quality.

A

    (i)   *a* when followed by a nasal consonant, as in *chant, âme, agneau,* is pronounced [ã] from about 1000.

    The modern French [ɑ̃] should not be used before the seventeenth century.

    (ii) *ai* when followed by a nasal consonant, as in *faim, aime,* is pronounced [ãĩ] to about 1100, [ɛ̃ĩ] to about 1500, thereafter [ɛ̃] or [ɛ] as in modern French.

          To 1100:   [ãĩ]
          1100-1500:   [ɛ̃ĩ]
          After 1500: [ɛ̃], [ɛ]

E

    (i) *e* when followed by a nasal consonant, as in *temps, vent,* is pronounced [ɛ̃] to about 1050, thereafter [ã].

The modern French [ɑ̃] should not be used before the seventeenth century.

Note that the vowel in the third person verb-ending *-ent* was not nasalized, but should be treated as 'feminine' *e*.

    (ii) *ei* when followed by a nasal consonant, as in *sein, pleine,* is pronounced [ɛ̃ĭ] from about 1150 to 1500, thereafter [ɛ̃] or [ɛ] as in modern French.

> To 1150:   [ɛi]
> 1150-1500: [ɛ̃ĭ]
> After 1500: [ɛ̃], [ɛ]

I

    (i) This vowel was probably not nasalized before 1350, and then not very strongly. When *i* is followed by a nasal consonant, as in *vigne, prince, fin,* it should be pronounced [ĩ] in the 15th century. From about 1500, in words like *vigne, voisine,* where the nasal vowel is followed by a nasal consonant **and another vowel,** the pure vowel [i] is pronounced; in words like *prince, vin,* the nasalized vowel remains and is pronounced [ɛ̃] as in modern French.

> To 1350:   [i]
> 1350-1500: [ĩ]
> After 1500: [i], [ɛ̃]

    (ii) *ie* when followed by a nasal consonant, as in *bien, vient, viennent,* is pronounced [ie] to about 1250, then [jɛ̃] to about 1500, thereafter [jɛ̃] or [jɛ] as in modern French. The pronunciation [jã] was used widely in provincial and popular Parisian speech from about 1300.

> To 1250:   [ie]
> 1250-1500: [jɛ̃], [jã] in provincial and popular speech
> After 1500: [jɛ̃], [jɛ], [jã] in provincial and popular speech

O

(i) *o,* when followed by a nasal consonant, as in *donner, ombre,* is nasalized from about 1200. The sound was generally [ɔ̃] in Francien and [ũ] in the provinces, but both sounds seem to have been current in Parisian speech in the 16th century. See the notes accompanying the examples in part 3 and on the companion cassette.

(ii) *oi,* when followed by a nasal consonant, as in *loin, point,* is pronounced [uɛ̃] from about 1150. The modern French [wɛ̃] may be found in rhymes, especially in Parisian poets, from 1300, but is not accepted as correct until about 1600.

> 1150-1300: [uɛ̃]
> 1300-1600: [uɛ̃], [wɛ̃]
> After 1600: [wɛ̃]

U

Like [i], the vowel [y] was nasalized late, and then not very strongly. When *u* is followed by a nasal consonant, as in *lune, un, fortune,* it should be pronounced [ỹ] in the 15th century. From about 1500, in words like *lune, une,* where the nasal vowel is followed by a nasal consonant **and another vowel,** the pure vowel [y] is pronounced; in words like *un, humble,* the nasalized vowel [ỹ] remains the correct form until the 17th century, but the modern French [œ̃] begins to be used from about 1550.

> To 1400: [y]
> 1400-1500: [ỹ]
> 1500-1550: [y], [ỹ]
> 1550-1600: [y], [ỹ], [œ̃]

CONSONANTS

Not all consonants require special mention; in the absence of comment, it may be assumed that pronunciation was fairly similar to that of today.

Final consonants are a special case, whose complicated history is difficult to treat within the simple terms of this guide. Generally speaking, all final consonants were pronounced to about 1250 and then became mute except when sounded to mark a liaison or the end of a phrase or sentence. Poets of the 14th and 15th centuries freely use words whose final consonant may or may not be sounded according to the demands of the rhyme, and performers should take their cue from the poetry rather than from linguistic history.

In the 16th century, however, attempts were made, sometimes successfully, to revert to the practice of sounding final consonants, and this habit became at the time a mark of correct, or hyper-correct, language and may be used in performing the more formal works of the period.

c, as in *cité, ciel,* is pronounced [ts] to about 1250, thereafter [s] as in modern French.

ch, as in *chanter, cher,* is pronounced [tʃ] to about 1250, thereafter [ʃ] as in modern French.

g followed by *e* or *i,* as in *rouge, argent, gîte,* is pronounced [dʒ] to about 1250, thereafter [ʒ] as in modern French.

gu is a spelling variant for *g* in words like *guerre, guet, guarder,* and is pronounced [g].

h, in *all* words marked * in modern dictionaries to indicate 'aspirate h', was fully aspirate (as in English *house*) in correct speech until the 17th century. Examples: *haïr, honte, hardi.*

j, as in *jaloux, joie,* is pronounced [dʒ] to about 1250, thereafter [ʒ] as in modern French.

l: note that old spellings such as *albe, altre, chevels, els* (= *eux*), do not represent pronunciation; [l] followed by another consonant had become [u] by 1150, and pronunciation should follow the indications for [au], [eu], etc., given above.

Words spelt with *il* or *ill,* as in *travail, feuille, vieillir,* are pronounced [λ] as in Italian *figlio* or Spanish *llamar.* The modern French [j] should not be used.

Final *l,* as in *avril, péril,* is not pronounced 1300-1500 except in liaison, but was often restored in 16th century correct speech.

r is pronounced as a trill with the tip of the tongue on the teeth-ridge as in modern Spanish or Italian. The modern French uvular [R] should not be used except in 16th century texts where it is specifically intended to convey colloquial Parisian speech.

Final *r* is not pronounced from about 1300 except in liaison. Note that this applies not only to verb infinitives, nouns, and adjectives in *-er* and *-ier* such as *chanter, berger, papier, premier,* but also to infinitives in *-ir,* and to nouns and adjectives in *-eur, -oir,* and *-our* such as *trompeur, miroir, carrefour.* Although modern French now pronounces some of these words with a final uvular [R], in medieval and Renaissance times the final *r* in such words was silent except in liaison. However, verb infinitives in *-oir,* such as *avoir,* retain their final *r* throughout the period covered by this guide.

rr is pronounced as a double consonant in words like *courrai, mourrai.*

s followed by *f, l, m,* as in *desfaite, isle, blasme,* was not pronounced after about 1050.

s followed by *t, k, p,* as in *feste, escuyer, espouser,* was not pronounced after about 1150.

Although the *s* in such words often persists in spelling throughout medieval and Renaissance times, it should not be pronounced.

Final *s* is pronounced to about 1200 and is thereafter silent except in liaison, when it is pronounced [z]. Note that this applies to words such as *fils, jadis, mars;* the modern French pronunciation with sounded *s* should not be used.

x, in early texts, represents the sounds [us] at the end of a word; thus *chevax* should be pronounced [tʃɛvaus]. From about 1300, however, *u* and sometimes also *l* were restored in spelling, and final *x* is no more than a spelling variant of *s;* thus the pronunciation of *chevaux, chevaulx,* should follow the guidance for [au] above.

z, as in verb-endings such as *aimez,* is pronounced [ts] to about 1225, [s] to about 1300, and is thereafter silent except in liaison, when it is pronounced [z].

PROVENÇAL (LANGUE D'OC)

Though 'Provençal' is a generally recognized term, 'Langue d'Oc' is perhaps more apt to describe the language of this very extensive region, whose northern boundary runs roughly through Bordeaux, Limoges, Roanne, and Grenoble. Its south and south-eastern limits are the Pyrenees and the Mediterranean, though in the early period Catalonia shared with it many cultural and linguistic features, and poets in Italy also used its language as a medium. It is a much larger area than that understood today as 'Provence', and many of its poets came from Gascony, Languedoc, Limousin, and Périgord. For almost two centuries (1100-1300) it produced lyric poetry unrivalled in grace and sophistication and strongly unified in linguistic and poetic convention.

The language of the troubadours must be understood as a literary idiom used by poets of widely different geographical and social origin, and varying little throughout the period; it might be compared to the formal language of Welsh poetry, still in use today yet not necessarily corresponding to the forms of everyday speech.

Over four hundred and fifty troubadours are known to us by name, and there were certainly more of whom no trace remains. The extreme elaboration of most of the poetic forms they used, with complicated repeated rhymes often deliberately chosen for their difficulty, gives an important hint to the modern executant: on the one hand 'double' or alternative forms may be found for reasons of metre or rhyme; on the other hand every effort must be made to reproduce in performance the identity of rhyme in which the poet took so much pride.

The notes on the following two pages were compiled with the help of Professor J. H. Marshall.

Vowels

A

(i)   In general, *a* is pronounced [ɑ].

(ii)   When *a* was followed by a Latin *n*, which usually disappeared, as in *pa* ('bread'), *ca* ('dog'), *lonhda* ('distant'), it had a different sound, which was probably half way between [ɑ] and [o].

(iii)   *au* is a diphthong as in *causa, aur, paraula.*

E

(i)   Provençal uses [e], as in *pres* ('taken'), *me* ('me'), and [ɛ], as in *pres* ('near'), *pe* ('foot').

(ii)   When *e* was followed by a Latin *n*, which usually disappeared, as in *be* ('well'), *ve* ('he comes'), it is pronounced [e].

(iii)   Final *e*, as in *paire, ribatge*, is pronounced [ɛ] (not [ə]).

(iv)   *eu* is a diphthong, as in the first person singular pronoun *ieu* or *eu* ([jɛu] or [ɛu]).

I

As in modern French *fine.*

O

(i)   Provençal uses [ɔ], as in *oc, vol,* and [o], as in *amor, lonh.*

(ii)   When *o* was followed by a Latin *n*, which usually disappeared, as in *bo, bona* ('good'), it is pronounced [o].

U

As in modern French *dur.*

There are no nasalized vowels.

CONSONANTS

    (i) *s* when followed by a consonant is pronounced, as in *castel, estela, esperanza.*

    (ii) Final consonants are pronounced, as in *cors, cantar, mort, amic, camp, amanz.*

    c final is usually [k], as in *ric* ('powerful'), *oc* ('yes'), *amic* ('friend').

    g final is [ʃ], as in *fag* ('deed'), *gaug* ('joy').

    z final is [ts], as in *amanz.*

    (iii) Before *e* and *i*, *c* is pronounced [ts] or [s], as in *cen* ('hundred'), and *g* is pronounced [dʒ], as in *gen* ('people'); before other vowels, they are respectively [k] and [g], as in *cantar* ('to sing'), and *gan* ('glove').

    (iv) *h* is not pronounced. The spellings *lh, nh* represent [λ], [ɲ]. [λ] is also spelt *ll* or *ill,* and [ɲ] *gn* or *ign.*

ALTERNATIVE FORMS

    These are used for metre or rhyme, or occasionally as a whim. A few examples only are given; the prime consideration for the performer should be to preserve identity of rhyme.

    (i) [tʃ] or [k]: the very common words *chantar, chant, chanzo* should be pronounced [tʃ], while other words beginning in *ch-* have [k].

    (ii) [g] or [dʒ]: *gaug, gauch* (happiness, rejoicing) should be pronounced [gauʃ]; *joi* (ecstasy of love) should be pronounced [dʒɔi].

    (iii) Single vowels or diphthongs: e.g., *velh* or *vielh, foc* or *fuoc, fruch* or *fruit.*

    (iv) Final [l] or [λ]: e.g., *caval* or *cavalh.*

    (v) Final *n* is frequently omitted: e.g., *pan* or *pa, razon* or *razo, bon* or *bo, un(s)* or *u(s).*

PICARD

Before the Renaissance, this term applied to a very large area, including to the south Beauvais, Soissons, and Laon, and to the north Tournai, Mons, and Hainault, which are now in Belgium.

In the 12th and 13th centuries the region's commercial and industrial wealth grew, especially from textiles, and especially in its rich self-governing towns such as Arras. From a literary point of view, the most productive period was the 13th and 14th centuries, when lyric and narrative poetry, drama, history, didactic works, and *fabliaux* were written.

The more important variations of pronunciation are set out below; where no comment is made, it may be assumed that the forms would be similar to the 'standard', that is, to the Francien forms.

VOWELS

(i)   Many words containing a diphthong are simplified in Picard to a single vowel, usually, though not always, the first, e.g., *fare* for *faire, bos* [bɔs] for *bois.*

(ii)   The pronunciation [iau] for [ɛau] or [ɛu] is very characteristic of Picard, as in *biaus, aigniaus, chiaus* (= *ceux*). From about 1300 [iau] becomes [jao].

CONSONANTS

(i)   Picard [k], spelt *c, q, qu, k,* replaces Francien [tʃ], spelt *ch,* e.g., *canter* for *chanter, cartre* for *chartre, karue* for *charrue, quemin* for *chemin, rike* for *riche.*

(ii)   Picard [tʃ], spelt *ch,* replaces Francien [ts], spelt *c,* e.g., *chité* for *cité, chil* and *chist* for the demonstratives *cil* and *cist, merchi* for *merci, justiche* for *justice, noches* for *noces.*

(iii) Picard [g], spelt *g*, replaces Francien [dʒ], spelt *g*, *j*, e.g., *gambon* for *jambon*, *geter* for *jeter*.

(iv) Picard final *t* continues to be pronounced in the 13th century after it has become silent in Francien, as in *piet*, *marchiet*.

(v) Picard [s] replaces Francien final [ts] in words such as *asés*, *tos*, *dolans*, and especially in verb-endings such as *priés*.

(vi) Picard [w] replaces Francien initial [g], e.g. *wardes* for *guardez*, *wage* for *gage*, *Warniers* for *Garnier*.

(vii) Picard [au], [av], replace Francien [ab] in suffixes, e.g., *honoraule* for *honorable*, *caritavle* for *charitable*.

(viii) 'Aspirate h' is strongly pronounced.

Other Special Forms

(i) *le*, *se*, for *la*, *sa*, etc., as feminine forms.

(ii) *men*, *ten*, for *mon*, *ton*, etc., as possessive forms.

(iii) *nos*, *no*, and *vos*, *vo*, for *nostre*, *nos*, etc., as plural possessive forms.

(iv) *jou* [dʒu] for *je* as first person pronoun.

(v) Many first person singular verbs end in -*c* or -*ch*, pronounced [tʃ], e.g., *perc*, *fach*, *commenc*.

(vi) Many first person plural verbs end in -*iemmes* or -*iens* for -*ions*, e.g., *feriemmes*, *deviens*.

(vii) Words like *fils*, *gentils*, are pronounced [ius], often spelt *ix*, for Francien [is].

NORMAN

This term applies to the north-western area, extending roughly from the Seine estuary westwards to Brittany and southwards to the Loire. Linguistically it is less sharply characterized than Picard, with which it shares certain features, such as:

(i) [k] for [tʃ], as in *canter* for Francien *chanter,* *camp* for Francien *champ.*

(ii) [iau] for [ɛau], as in *biau* for Francien *beau.*

(iii) strong 'aspirate h'.

Other characteristics are:

(iv) The nasal vowel [ãĩ], as in *aime, faim,* became [ɛ̃] as in modern French, from about 1150.

(v) *ei,* as in the modern French *foi, moi,* etc., became [ɛ] instead of [wɛ] (see the notes above on *ei* and *oi*). The pronunciation [ɛ] seems to have been a recognized Norman feature in the 16th century.

(vi) Final *r* was pronounced in words like *chanter, monsieur,* after it had disappeared from 'standard' French.

(vii) Nasal vowels and consonants were strongly pronounced. The vowel *a* when nasalized, as in *grand, Normand,* had the modern [ɑ̃].

In very early texts the following verb-forms sometimes occur; they usually disappear during the 13th century.

(i) Imperfect tense endings spelt *-oue,* etc., as in *chantoue,* pronounced [ɔuə].

(ii) Subjunctive endings spelt *-ge,* as in *plange, alge,* pronounced [dʒə].

(iii) First person plural endings in *-um* or *-un* instead of *-ons,* as in *ferum,* pronounced [um].

BIBLIOGRAPHY

GENERAL HISTORIES OF THE LANGUAGE:

E. & J. Bourciez, *Phonétique française, étude historique,* Paris, 1967.
A. Ewert, *The French Language,* London, 1933.
P. Fouché, *Phonétique historique du français,* 3 vols., Paris, 1952-61.
M. K. Pope, *From Latin to modern French,* Manchester, 1934.
C. Thurot, *De la Prononciation française depuis le commencement du XVIe siècle,* 2 vols., Paris, 1881-83.

PROVENÇAL:

E. Bourciez, *Éléments de linguistique romane,* 4th edn., Paris, 1946.
J. Anglade, *Grammaire de l'ancien provençal,* Paris, 1921.

PICARD:

C. T. Gossen, *Petite grammaire de l'ancien Picard,* Paris, 1951.
F. J. Warne (ed), Jean Bodel: *Le Jeu de Saint Nicolas,* Oxford, 1951.

Part 2

CHART

The following chart can be used to look up the pronunciation for a text of any specific date. For instance, if a chanson by Dufay of c. 1450 is to be performed, a glance at the chart will show the state of French pronunciation in 1450.

The chart lists only differences from modern French. Thus, if a spelling is not listed, it should be treated as pronounced as it would be in modern educated Parisian French.

The chart does not cover Provençal, Picard, or Norman.

Vowels

	a when followed by an *s* that becomes silent, as in *pas, mât, âne*	*ai* *faire, mais, raison*	*ai* in verb endings *j'aimai*
1100		[ai]	[ai]
1200			[ɛ]
1300	[a]	[ɛ]	
1400			[e]
1500			
1600	[ɑ]		

* for details, see the text above.

32

au	*ei*	*eu*	*e* final or in monosyllables	*eau*
aube, autre	*mei, curteis*	*fleur, cheveux*	*père, je*	*beau*
↑ [au] ↓ ―――― ↑ [ao] ↓ ―――― ↑ [o] ↓	↑ [ei] ―――― [ɔi] ―――― ↑ [uɛ] ↓ ―――― ↑↑ [wɛ], [ɛ], [wa] * ↓	↑ [ɛu] ↓ ―――― ↑ [œ] ↓	↑ as in English *get* ↓ ―――― ↑ as in English *sofa* ↓ ―――― ↑ as in modern French ↓	↑ [ɛau] ↓ ―――― ↑ [ɛao] ↓ ―――― ↑ [əo] ↓

	ie	*oi*	*ui*
	pied, fièvre	*voix, joie, gloire*	*nuit, conduire*
1100	[ie]	[oi]	[yi]
1200	[je]	[uɛ], [wɛ] *	[ɥi]
1300			
1400	as in modern French	[wɛ], [ɛ], [wa] *	
1500			
1600			

* for details, see the text above.

ASAL VOWELS

a + nasal consonant *chant, âme, agneau*	*ai* + nasal consonant *faim, aime*	*e* + nasal consonant *temps, vent, femme*	*ei* + nasal consonant *sein, pleine*
↑ [ã] and the consonant ↓ ――― [ã], [a] * ↓	↑ [ɛ̃ɪ] and the consonant ↓ ――― ↑ [ɛ̃], [ɛ] * ↓	↑ [ã] and the consonant ↓ ――― [ã], [a] * ↓	↑ [eɪ] and the consonant ――― ↓ ↑ [ɛ̃ɪ] and the consonant ↓ ――― ↑ [ɛ̃], [ɛ] * ↓

(vertical scale at left: 1100, 1200, 1300, 1400, 1500, 1600)

NASAL VOWELS

	i + nasal consonant *vigne, fin*	*ie* + nasal consonant *bien, viennent*	*o* + nasal consonant *ombre, donner*
1100	↑	↑	↑
1200	[i] and the consonant	[ie] and the consonant ↓	[o] and the consonant ↓
1300	↓	↑ [jẽ], [jã] and the consonant *	[ɔ̃], [ũ], and the consonant *
1400	↑ [ī] and the consonant		
1500	↓ [i], [ɛ̃] *	↓ [jẽ], [jã], [jɛ] *	↓ [ɔ̃], [ũ] *
1600	↓	↓	↓

* for details, see the text above.

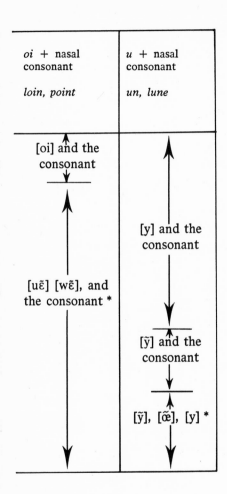

oi + nasal consonant	*u* + nasal consonant
loin, point	*un, lune*

[oi] and the consonant

[uɛ̃] [wɛ̃], and the consonant *

[y] and the consonant

[ỹ] and the consonant

[ỹ], [œ̃], [y] *

CONSONANTS

	c + e, i	ch	g + e, i	initial h, in words marked * in modern dictionaries
	cité, ciel	chanter, cher	rouge, argent	haïr, honte
1100	↑	↑	↑	↑
	[ts]	[tʃ]	[dʒ]	
1200	↓	↓	↓	
	—	—	—	
1300	↑	↑	↑	[h]
1400				
	[s]	[ʃ]	[ʒ]	
1500				
1600	↓	↓	↓	↓

* for details, see the text above.

j	*r.*	*z* final
jaloux *joie*	*rose,* *avril,* *finir*	*aimez*

↕ [dʒ]	↕	↕ [ts]
───		─── [s]
↕ [ʒ]	[r] (not [R]) *	───
		↕ silent except in liaison

Part 3

EXAMPLES

The following twelve examples date from between 1100 and 1600. They include extracts from an epic and a play, while the rest are poems that were set to music in their own time. These have been chosen because their musical settings are all readily available in modern editions.

Each poem or extract is accompanied by a modern English version prepared for this book, and by explanatory notes on the content, language, metre, and music.

A cassette is available from the publisher on which all twelve examples are spoken with the original pronunciation, and on which six of them are also sung in musical settings of their period.

CONTENTS

	Cassette:
1. **La Chanson de Roland:** the opening lines; the death of Roland; parts of Charlemagne's lament on the death of Roland Norman, early 12th century	Spoken
2. **'Be m'an perdut lai enves Ventadorn',** a song with words and music by the troubadour Bernard de Ventadorn Provençal, about 1180	Spoken; and then the 1st, 3rd, and 6th stanzas, and the envoi, sung
3. Part of a tavern scene from the miracle play **Le Jeu de Saint Nicolas** by Jean Bodel Picard, about 1200	Spoken
4. **'On parole de batre et de vanner',** an anonymous motet Francien, about 1260	Spoken
5. **'Dieus soit en cheste maison',** a Christmas song with words and music by Adam de la Hale Francien/Picard, about 1280	Spoken and then sung
6. **'Amours et ma dame aussi',** a rondeau with words and music by Adam de la Hale Francien/Picard, about 1280	Spoken
7. **'Plus dure qu'un dÿamant',** a virelai with words and music by Machaut About 1350	Spoken; and then the first section sung

8. 'Je ne suis plus telx que soloye', an anonymous rondeau which was set to music by Dufay About 1430	Spoken
9. 'Avez point veu la Perronnelle', a strophic song whose words and music are both anonymous About 1490	Spoken and then sung
10. 'Nous sommes de l'ordre de Saint Babouin', a strophic song whose words are anonymous and which was set to music by Compère About 1500	Spoken; and then the first stanza sung
11. 'La nuyt froyde et sombre', two stanzas of an ode by du Bellay which were set to music by Lassus 1549	Spoken and then sung
12. 'Amour et Mars sont presque d'une sorte', a sonnet by Ronsard 1560	Spoken

1

La Chanson de Roland: the opening lines; the death of
Roland; and parts of Charlemagne's lament on the death
of Roland.

Norman, early 12th century.

Carles li reis, nostre emperere magnes,
Set anz tuz pleins ad estét en Espaigne,
Tresqu'en la mer cunquist la tere altaigne.
N'i ad castel ki devant lui remaigne,
Mur ne citét n'i est remés a fraindre,
Fors Sarraguce, ki est en une muntaigne;
Li reis Marsilie la tient ki Deu nen aimet,
Mahumet sert e Apollin recleimet;
Ne·s poet guarder que mals ne l'i ateignet.

Li reis Marsilie esteit en Sarraguce,   10
Alez en est en un verger suz l'umbre,
Sur un perrun de marbre bloi se culched,
Envirun lui plus de vint milie humes.
Il en apelet e ses dux e ses cuntes:
'Oëz, seignurs, quel pecchét nus encumbret:
Li empereres Carles de France dulce
En cest païs nos est venuz cunfundre.
Jo nen ai ost qui bataille li dunne,
Ne n'ai tel gent ki la sue derumpet:
Cunseilez mei cume mi savie hume,   20
Si me guarisez e de mort e de hunte.'
N'i ad paien ki un sul mot respundet,
Fors Blancandrins de Castel de Valfunde.

———

Li quens Rollant se jut desuz un pin,
Envers Espaigne en ad turnét sun vis;
De plusurs choses a remembrer li prist:
De tantes teres cum li bers conquist,

De dulce France, des humes de sun lign,
De Carlemagne, sun seignor ki·l nurrit;
Ne poet müer n'en plurt e ne suspirt;
Mais lui meïsme ne volt mettre en ubli,
Cleimet sa culpe, si priet Deu mercit:
'Veire Patene, ki unkes ne mentis,   10
Seint Lazaron de mort resurrexis
E Danïel des leons guaresis,
Guaris de mei l'anme de tuz perilz
Pur les pecchez que en ma vie fis!'
Sun destre guant a Deu en puroffrit,
Seint Gabrïel de sa main l'ad pris.
Desur sun braz teneit le chef enclin,
Juntes ses mains est alét a sa fin.
Deus tramist sun angle Cherubin,
Ensembl'od li seint Michel del Peril;   20
Ensembl'od els sent Gabrïel i vint,
L'anme del cunte portent en pareïs.

———

'Ami Rollant, deus metet t'anme en flors
En pareïs entre les glorïus!
Cum en Espaigne venis a mal seignur!
Jamais n'ert jurn, de tei n'aie dulur.
Cum decarrat ma force e ma baldur!
Nen avrai ja ki sustienget m'onur;
Suz ciel ne quid aveir ami un sul;
Se jo ai parenz, nen i ad nul si proz.'
Trait ses crignels pleines ses mains amsdous;
Cent milie Franc en unt si grant dulur,   10
Nen i ad cel ki durement ne plurt.

'Ami Rollant, jo m'en irai en France.
Cum jo serai a Loün en ma chambre,
De plusurs regnes vendrunt li hume estrange,
Demanderunt: "U est li quens cataignes?"
Jo lur dirrai qu'il est morz en Espaigne.

A grant dulur tendrai puis mun reialme:
Jamais n'ert jur que ne plur ne n'en pleigne.'

(Charles the King, our great emperor, has been full seven years in Spain. He has conquered the highlands as far as the sea; there is no castle still standing before him, no wall or city remains to be breached, save Saragossa, which stands upon a mountain. King Marsilion holds it; he is no servant of God; it is Mohammed he honours, and Apollo he invokes. But he cannot protect himself from the fate that will reach him there.

King Marsilion sat in Saragossa. He has gone into an orchard, in the shade; he is reclining on a dais of blue marble; around him are more than twenty thousand men. He calls his dukes and his counts: 'Now hear, my lords, what evil besets us. Charles, the emperor of fair France, has come to this land to overcome us. I have no army to give him battle, no forces to shatter his. Give me counsel as my trusted vassals and save me from death and shame.' No pagan says a single word in reply, save Blancandrin from Castel de Valfunde.

———

Count Roland lay down beneath a pinetree, his face turned towards Spain. The memory of many things came to him: the many lands he conquered as a knight, fair France, the men of his line, Charlemagne his lord who brought him up. He cannot help but weep and sigh. But he does not wish to forget his duty to himself; he confesses his sins and prays to God for mercy: 'True Father, who never lied, who didst raise Saint Lazarus from the dead and save Daniel from the lions, save my soul from all dangers in respect of the sins I have committed in my life.' He held out his right glove to God; Saint Gabriel took it from his hand. His head bowed over his arm; with hands joined in prayer he went to his end. God sent down his angel Cherubim, and with him Saint Michael of the Peril of the sea, and with these two Saint Gabriel came to him. They bear the count's soul to paradise.

———

'Roland my friend, God keep your soul in flowers, in paradise among the glorious. With what a wretched lord you came to Spain! There will not be a day when I do not grieve for you. How my force and ardour will decline! I shall have no one to uphold my honour. I think I have not a single friend under heaven; if I have kinsfolk, there is none so valiant.' He tears his hair with both his hands; a hundred thousand Frenchmen are in such grief there is not one who does not weep most bitterly.

'Roland my friend, I shall go back to France. When I am at Laon in my hall, the foreign vassals will come from many lands, and ask: "Where is the chieftain count?" I shall tell them he is dead in Spain. In great sorrow I shall henceforth keep my kingdom. There will not be a day when I do not weep and lament.')

The *Chanson de Roland* is probably the earliest, and certainly the greatest, of the eighty to a hundred epic poems or *chansons de geste* popular from about the 11th to the 13th centuries. Their usual subjects are feudal or religious war, often set in a previous age such as that of Charlemagne, and their themes are treachery and loyalty, fidelity to God and one's lord, and the quest for glory and heroic deeds. This poem contains them all.

The poem is written in groups of lines, called *laisses.* They do not rhyme, but assonate: that is, the last stressed vowel of each line is identical. The assonating vowel can of course be followed by a 'mute' *e* as in the first *laisse,* and poetic licence allows some approximations to pass. The lines are of ten syllables, with a strong pause or caesura after the fourth syllable; this may also be followed by a 'mute' *'e,* as in line 6 of the first *laisse.*

The poems were originally indeed *chansons* or songs, performed to music. However, it is not certain how this was done — whether they were actually sung to a melody, or declaimed or intoned to an accompaniment.

We have chosen three famous parts of the epic: the opening lines, the death of Roland, and parts of Charlemagne's lament on the death of Roland. In F. Whitehead's edition (Oxford, Blackwell, 1947), they are lines 1-23, 2375-96, and 2898-2915.

It is impossible in this context to do more than hint at the most striking aspects of the *Chanson de Roland.* In the first extract, notice the masterly concision of the opening lines, introducing the emperor, the time, place and purpose of the tale, the name and fell nature of the enemy; the use of direct speech whenever possible; and the use (as in line 9) of foreboding or prophetic lines which create a sense of ordained pattern while preserving for the characters their freedom to act.

The second extract tells of the death of Roland, the faithful warrior, after the Battle of Roncevaux. His dying thoughts are of the martial exploits achieved for his earthly lord Charlemagne. As he confesses his sins aloud (there being no priest remaining) God despatches messengers, two archangels Gabriel and Michael (the latter here linked with Mont St. Michel), and 'Cherubin', often taken as a proper name designating the fourth archangel Uriel, to receive the glove he offers, and his soul. The glove is a feudal gesture of service, and so the feudal structure is transferred literally to a new dimension, from earth to heaven.

The third extract is part of the formal lament pronounced by Charlemagne over the dead at Roncevaux. It illustrates epic hyperbole — Charlemagne tears his hair, a hundred thousand Frenchmen weep bitterly — and also the device known as *laisses similaires,* in which a number of *laisses* develop the same incident or theme, often linked by words in common, here by the invocation 'Ami Rollant.'

Debate over the place of composition, date and authorship of this famous poem has raged as keenly as the battle of Roncevaux itself. The author is not known; the date is probably the early years of the 12th century, though the manuscript was copied and revised later in that century; and the place is indicated by the language, which shows Norman and Western features. Examples of these would be the pronunciation of words like *Carles* and *castel* with [k] not [tʃ], and a preference for [u] instead of [o] in words like *plurt* and *flors.*

When spoken, the old language before about 1250 would seem somewhat emphatic to a modern ear. The final consonants of words were normally all sounded, and the words themselves were not run together in phrases or breath-groups as is now the case. On the other hand, there were fewer nasal vowels, and more high vowels (for example in words like *un, vin, reis*), so that the overall pitch of the language would have been higher than the French of today. Other distinguishing sounds in so early a piece would be: words like *citét, cest, France* would have [ts] not [s]; *jo* (= *je*) is pronounced [dʒo]; *z* at the end of words like *anz, alez, cunseilez,* etc., is [ts]; the *a* in *anz* etc., and the *e* in *en* etc., would both be [ã]; words like *reis, poet, ai, tei,* were pronounced with diphthongs as spelt; words like *milie* (= *mille*), *cunseilez, peril,* had [ʎ]; words like *dulce, del* (= *du*), *reialme,* had [u] where the spelling still shows *l*; verb endings in words like *ad* and *priet* were pronounced [θ] as in English *thin,* but forms like *cunquist, tient, prist,* would still retain [t].

2

'Be m'an perdut lai enves Ventadorn,' a song with words and
music by the troubadour Bernard de Ventadorn.

Provençal, about 1180.

Be m'an perdut lai enves Ventadorn
tuih mei amic, pois ma donna no m'ama;
et es be dreihz que ja mais lai no torn,
c'ades estai vas me salvatj'e grama.
Ve·us per que·m fai semblan irat e morn:
car en s'amor me deleih e·m sojorn!
Ni de ren als no·s rancura ni·s clama.

Aissi co·l peis qui s'eslaiss' el cadorn
e no·n sap mot, tro que s'es pres en l'ama,
m'eslaissei eu vas trop amar un jorn,   10
c'anc no·m gardei, tro fui en mei la flama,
que m'art plus fort, no·m feira focs de forn;
e ges per so no·m posc partir un dorn,
aissi·m te pres d'amors e m'aliama.

No·m meravilh si s'amors me te pres,
que genser cors no crei qu'el mon se mire:
bels e blancs es, e frescs e gais e les
e totz aitals com eu volh e dezire.
No posc dir mal de leis, que non i es;
qu'e·l n'agra dih de joi, s'eu li saubes;   20
mas no li sai, per so m'en lais de dire.

Totz tems volrai sa onor e sos bes
e·lh serai om et amics e servire,
e l'amarai, be li plass' o be·lh pes,
c'om no pot cor destrenher ses aucire.
No sai domna, volgues o no volgues,

si·m volia, c'amar no la pogues.
Mas totas res pot om en mal escrire.

A las autras sui aissi eschazutz;
la cals se vol me pot vas se atraire,   30
per tal cove que no·m sia vendutz
l'onors ni·l bes que m'a en cor a faire;
qu'enoyos es preyars, pos er perdutz;
per me·us o dic, que mals m'en en vengutz,
car traït m'a la bela de mal aire.

En Proensa tramet jois e salutz
e mais de bes c'om no lor sap retraire;
e fatz esfortz, miracles e vertutz,
car eu lor man de so don non ai gaire,
qu'eu non ai joi, mas tan can m'en adutz   40
mos Bels Vezers e'n Fachura, mos drutz,
e'n Alvernhatz, lo senher de Belcaire.

Mos Bels Vezers, per vos fai Deus vertutz
tals c'om no·us ve que no si' ereubutz
dels bels plazers que sabetz dir e faire.

(They have quite lost me, all my friends away towards Ventadorn, since my lady does not love me; and it is indeed right that I should never return there, for still she remains cruel and harsh towards me. See why she shows herself to me angry and unsmiling: it is because I delight in and persist in love for her! For no other reason is she filled with rancour and complaint.

Just like the fish which swims headlong towards the bait and knows nothing until it is caught on the hook, I rushed headlong one day into loving too much without ever paying heed, until I was in the midst of that flame which burns me more fiercely than would the fire of a furnace; but for all that I cannot move a hand's breadth away, so firmly does she hold me captive and bind me with love.

I am not amazed if her love holds me captive, for I believe no fairer form is to be seen in the world: beautiful and white it is, young and pleasing and smooth, and exactly such as I wish and desire. I can speak no ill of her, for there is none in her; for I would joyfully have spoken ill of her, if I had known any in her; but I know of none in her, for which reason I refrain from speaking any.

Always I shall strive for her honour and her good and shall be her liege-man and lover and serving-man, and I shall love her, whether it please her or anger her, for a man cannot constrain his heart without killing. I know of no lady, whether she would or no, whom if I had the will I could not love. But people can ascribe all things to a bad motive.

Thus I am fallen to the lot of other women; whoever wants can draw me towards her, provided only that the honour and the good which she has in her heart to do me are not sold to me [i.e., are not the subject of bargaining], for imploring is burdensome if it is to be fruitless; it is from my own experience that I tell you this, for ill-fortune has come to me thereby, since that fair perfidious one betrayed my trust.

To Provence I send words of joy and salutations and more good things than can ever be told; and I strive, I perform wonders and miracles, for I send to them that of which I have but little, for I have no joy except as much as is brought me by my Bel Vezer (Fair Vision) and Sir Fachura (Enchanter) my friend and Sir Auvergnat, the lord of Beaucaire.

My Bel Vezer, through you God performs miracles, in that no one sees you without being uplifted by the fair pleasing words and deeds which you know how to speak and perform.)

(Translation supplied by Professor J. H. Marshall)

This is one of the best-known songs of the troubadour Bernard de Ventadorn, who lived in the late 12th century. In it, the poet declares his love and laments that it is not reciprocated.

The poetry of the troubadours had a profound influence on European literature up to our own time. Much of it survives, and much of the music too. Unfortunately, the rhythmic interpretation of the troubadour melodies remains a puzzle. The version recorded on the cassette accompanying this book is taken from Carl Parrish's *A Treasury of Early Music,* New York, 1959, no. 6; the reader should be warned, however, that this is only one of a number of possible rhythmic interpretations. There also exists a second melody for this poem; two interpretations of it are printed in the

e bele parleure

Historical Anthology of Music, edited by A. T. Davison and W. Apel, I (Harvard University Press), 1949, no. 18b.

For details about the pronunciation of troubadour poems, see the section on Provençal above. Notice the care taken with the rhymes, as commonly in troubadour poetry: in this poem, each pair of stanzas has two rhymes only.

3

Part of a tavern scene from the miracle play **Le Jeu de Saint Nicolas** by Jean Bodel.

Picard, about 1200.

RASOIRS

Or bevons plus, si parlons mains,
Car recouvrees sont nos pertes:
Les granges Dieu sont aouvertes;
Ne puet muer ne soions rique,
Car au tresor le roi d'Aufrique,
A coupe n'a hanap n'a nef
N'a mais ne serrure ne clef
Ne serjant qui le gart nule eure;
Ains gist uns mahommés deseure,
Ne sai ou de fust ou de pierre.   10
Ja par lui n'en ora espiere
Li rois, s'on li taut tout ou emble.
Ancui irons tout troi ensamble
Quant nous sarons qu'il en ert eure.

PINCEDÉS

Est che voirs, que Diex te sekeure?

RASOIRS

Est voirs? Oïl, par saint Jehan!
Car j'en oï crïer le ban
Qu'il n'iert ja mais hom qui le gait,
Mais qui en puist avoir, s'en ait!
Gardés s'on puet chi sus acroire.   20

(RASOIR: Now let's have more drink and less talk, for all our losses are made good. God's own stores are laid open. We can't help but be rich. For the King of Africa's treasure — goblets, tankards, vessels — has neither lock nor key nor sentry to guard it at any hour. Instead, there's an idol sitting on it — made of wood or stone, I don't know. The King will never get wind from that if everything is stolen and disappears. We'll all three go together, this very day, when we know the time's right.

PINCEDÉ: Is that true, so help you God?

RASOIR: True? Of course, by Saint John! I heard the crier give out that there'd be no one guarding it any more, and anyone who could get it could have it. So you can see that's good surety for borrowing.)

Jean Bodel's miracle play *Le Jeu de Saint Nicolas* was first performed in Arras on St. Nicholas' Eve (5 December), probably in 1200. The scene is a tavern at night: one of the three thieves, Rasoir, is reporting to his friends on a treasure that lies unguarded, ready for them to steal. Taken (by permission) from the edition by F. J. Warne, Oxford, Blackwell, 1951 (repr. 1972), pp. 32-3.

Picard forms include: [tʃ] for Francien [ts], as in *che* (line 15) for *ce,* and *chi sus* (line 20) for *ci* or *ici*; [s] for [ts] in the verb-ending of *gardés* (line 20); [au] for [ou] in *taut* ('take away') (line 12); pronunciation of final *t* in *puet, gart, taut, ait,* etc.

There are also two Picard rhymes. In lines 4-5 the rhyme *rique: Aufrique* shows the Picard [k] for [tʃ] in 'standard' *riche*; and in lines 10-11 the rhyme is actually in *-ire* and shows the word *pierre* ('stone') pronounced with the regional simplification to [i] and therefore rhyming with *espire* ('breath') (the copyist has written *espiere* to make the words look more similar, but they form a good Picard rhyme without assistance). On the other hand, the rhyme *emble: ensamble* in lines 12-13 uses the standard Francien form of the second word, whereas elsewhere Bodel has *ensanle* without [b], which is the more characteristic northern form.

Features common in Picard, but not exclusive to it, are the inconsistency in single and double consonants, as in *ora* (line 11) for *orra* ('will hear'), and the form *sarons* (line 14) for *savrons* ('will know').

The *h* of *hanap* (line 6) would be fully aspirated; *gardés* appears here with *g* but elsewhere in the play is spelt with *w* — pronunciation with [w] gives a stronger 'local accent.'

In line 4, *ne* meaning 'not' is pronounced [nə], whereas in lines 7-8 *ne* ... *ne* meaning 'neither ... nor' is pronounced [ne].

4

'**On parole de batre et de vanner**,' an anonymous motet.

Francien, about 1260.

I

On parole de batre et de vanner,
Et de föir et de hanner;
Mais ces deduis
Trop me desplaisent,
Car il n'est si bone vie
Que d'estre à aise,
De bon cler vin et de chapons,
Et d'estre aveuc bons compaignons,
Liés et joians,
Chantans, truffans, et amorous,   10
Et d'avoir quant c'on a mestier
Pour solacier
Beles dames à devis:
Et tout ce truev'on à Paris.

II

A Paris soir et matin
Truev'on bon pain et bon cler vin,
Bone char et bon poisson,
De toutes guises compaignons,
Sens soutil, grant baudour,
Biaus joiaus, dames d'ounour,
Et si truev'on bien entredeus
De menre feur pour homes desiteus.

III

Frese nouvele! Muere france!

(Some talk of threshing and winnowing, and digging and labouring. But these joys aren't my delight; for there's no life like being in comfort, with good clear wine and capons, and being with good companions, merry and rollicking, singing and joking and amorous, and having all you need to pleasure fair ladies to your heart's content. And all this you find in Paris.

In Paris by night and day you find good bread and good clear wine, good meat and fish, companions of every sort, sharp wits, great jollity, fine trinkets, ladies of honour — and you can find others too, however, costing less, for chaps hard up.

Fresh strawberries! Choice mulberries!)

This anonymous motet is about having a good time in Paris, with food, drink, friends, and female company. In the musical setting, the three French texts are sung *simultaneously* by three different voices.

The text is from Montpellier, Bibliothèque Universitaire, MS H 196, ff. 368 verso-369 verso. The music, which is found in the same source, is published in Y. Rokseth (ed.), *Polyphonies du XIIIe Siècle,* 4 vols., Paris, 1936-39, no. 319; in A. T. Davison and W. Apel, *Historical Anthology of Music,* I (Harvard University Press), 1949, no. 33b; and in Alec Harman, *Medieval and early Renaissance Music*, London, 1958, ex. 41.

The metre is irregular: the first line has ten syllables, and so has the last line of the second voice, but the main body of the poem uses eight-syllable (or perhaps two four-syllable) and seven-syllable lines. The rhymes vary also: most frequently they are in couplets, but there is a quatrain rhyming ABAB in lines 3-6, and two orphan lines 9 and 10. The alternation of masculine and feminine rhymes did not become a 'rule 'of French poetry until the Renaissance and is naturally absent here.

Because this is an early example of a long and seemingly inexhaustible line of poems in praise of Paris, and because of its fairly rumbustious subject-matter, we may consider it to illustrate popular Parisian French of the mid-13th century.

Final consonants such as *s (mais, ces), p (trop),* and *l (il, soutil),* would not be pronounced except for liaison, as in *liés et joians* (line 9), etc. Final *r,* however, would still be heard, as would the nasal consonants following nasalized vowels *(vanner, bone, sens,* etc.); and, at a pause or break in the content, all final consonants would be sounded, for example in *Paris* and *desiteus* at the end of the stanzas.

Of the nasal vowels, [ã] is present in for example *vanner, entredeus*; [ɛ̃] in *pain, bien,* etc.; and [ɔ̃] in *on, bone, bons,* etc. It will be remembered that both [ɔ] and [ũ] were pronunciations in current use right into the 16th and 17th centuries, but it seems that [ũ] was somewhat more provincial and vulgar, and [ɔ] was more likely to be found in the speech of Paris. The diphthongs in words like *mais, aise,* had become [ɛ] — indeed the word *frese* ('strawberry') is spelt with *e*; the *oi* in *joians, soir, poisson,* etc., was [wɛ]; and the *ie* in *liés, mestier, solacier,* was [je]. The sound variously spelt *ue* and *eu* in *truev'* (an early form of *trouve), entredeus, feur* ('cost'), *desiteus* ('needy'), *muere* (now *mûre,* 'mulberry'), was [œ]. The diphthong *au* in *baudour* ('delight') was still pronounced [au]; incidentally the form *biaus* — so often regarded as a northern regional form — in this Parisian poem shows the impossibility of trying to draw hard and fast lines between Parisian and provincial, correct and vulgar speech.

5

'**Dieus soit en cheste maison,**' a Christmas song with words
and music by Adam de la Hale.

Francien/Picard, about 1280.

> *Dieus soit en cheste maison,*
> *Et biens et goie a fuison.*

Nos sires Noueus
Nous envoie a ses amis,
Ch'est as amoureus
Et as courtois bien apris,
Pour avoir des pairesis
　A nohelison.

> *Dieus soit en cheste maison,*
> *Et biens et goie a fuison.*　　　　　　　　10

Nos sires est teus
Qu'il prieroit a envis,
Mais as frans honteus
Nous a en son lieu tramis,
Qui sommes de ses nouris
　Et si enfançon.

> *Dieus soit en cheste maison,*
> *Et biens et goie a fuison.*

(God be in this house, and wealth and joy in abundance!

Our lord of Christmas sends us to his friends, that's to say to
lovers and well-nurtured courtly folk, to earn a penny or two for
our Christmas songs. God be in this house, and wealth and joy in
abundance!

Our lord is such that he would be reluctant to entreat you, but
to honest gentlefolk he has sent us in his stead, we who are his
kinsfolk and his stock. God be in this house, and wealth and joy
in abundance!)

e bele parleure

This is one of the earliest known songs of Christmas waits. Words and music are by Adam de la Hale, who lived in Arras in the 13th century. The music is sung on the cassette accompanying this book. The text is taken from Adam de la Hale's *Lyric Works*, edited by Nigel Wilkins (American Institute of Musicology, 1967), pp. 58-9, where the music is also to be found.

Adam may have studied in Paris; in any case, his poems show a mixture of Francien and Picard forms.

There are few regional forms in this first poem (no. 5), other than *cheste, ch'est* (for *c'est*); the *h* of *honteus* would be strongly aspirate, and one could pronounce *maison, enfançon,* etc., with [ū] as a 'provincialism.' In lines 3 and 11, *nos sires* (for *nostre sires*) is Picard, though it is often found more widely. The spelling *eus* in *Noueus, amoureus,* etc., is probably the Francien [œ] — the Picard form would be [au].

The second poem (no. 6) shows rather more regionalisms, such as *merchi (= merci), biauté (= beauté), vo (= vostre), avés (= avez), mi (= moi), proi* [prwε] *(= prie).*

6

'Amours et ma dame aussi,' a rondeau with words and music
by Adam de la Hale.

Francien/Picard, about 1280.

> *Amours, et ma dame aussi,*
> *Jointes mains vous proi merchi.*
> Vo très grant biauté mar vi,
> *Amours, et ma dame aussi.*
> Se n'avés pité de mi,
> Vo très grans bontés mar vi.
> *Amours et ma dame aussi,*
> *Jointes mains vous proi merchi.*

(Love, and my lady too, I clasp my hands and beg for mercy.
Alas! that I ever saw your great beauty, Love, and my lady too.
Unless you have pity on me, alas! that I ever saw your kindliness.
Love, and my lady too, I clasp my hands and beg for mercy.)

The text is taken from Adam de la Hale's *Lyric Works,*
edited by Nigel Wilkins (American Institute of Musicology,
1967), pp. 54-5, where the music is also to be found. For
linguistic comments, see no. 5 above.

7

'**Plus dure qu'un dÿamant**,' a virelai with words and music by Machaut.

About 1350.

> Plus dure qu'un dÿamant
> Ne que pierre d'aÿmant
>   Est vo durté,
> Dame, qui n'avez pité
>   De vostre amant
> Qu'ociés en desirant
>   Vostre amitié.

Dame, vo pure biauté
Qui toutes passe, à mon gré,
  Et vo samblant   10
Simple et plein d'umilité,
De douceur fine paré,
  En sousriant,

Par un acqueil attraiant,
M'ont au cuer en regardant
  Si fort navré
Que ja mais joie n'avré,
  Jusques à tant
Que vo grace qu'il atent
  M'arez donné.   20

> Plus dure qu'un dÿamant
> Ne que pierre d'aÿmant
>   Est vo durté,
> Dame, qui n'avez pité
>   De vostre amant
> Qu'ociés en desirant
>   Vostre amitié.

J'ay humblement enduré
L'amoureus mal et porté
   En attendant   30
Vostre bonne volenté
Que j'ay en tous cas trouvé
   Dure et poingnant.

Et quant tous en vo commant
Suis, je me merveil comment
   Vostre bonté
M'a sa grace refusé,
   Quant en plourant
Vous ay et en souspirant
   Merci rouvé.   40

Plus dure qu'un dÿamant
Ne que pierre d'aÿmant
   Est vo durté,
Dame, qui n'avez pité
   De vostre amant
Qu'ocïés en desirant
   Vostre amitié.

Helas! Dame, conforté
Ne m'avez en ma grieté,
   Ne tant ne quant,   50
Eins m'avez desconforté,
Si que tout desconfort hé.
   Mais nonpourquant

J'ameray d'or en avant
Plus fort qu'onques mais, et quant
   Mort et miné
M'ara vostre cruauté
   Qui m'est trop grant,
Lors sera bien apparant
   Ma loyauté.   60

> *Plus dure qu'un dÿamant*
> *Ne que pierre d'aÿmant*
>   *Est vo durté,*
> *Dame, qui n'avez pité*
>   *De vostre amant*
> *Qu'ociés en desirant*
>   *Vostre amitié.*

(Harder than a diamond or lodestone is your harshness, Lady, who have no pity for your lover, whom you slay though he desires your love.

Lady, your perfect beauty, which exceeds any — to my mind — and your open look, full of humility, enhanced by sweet gentleness, have, smilingly, with their welcome wounded my heart so sorely as I gazed that I shall never more be happy until you have granted me the favour that my heart awaits. Harder than a diamond, &c.

I have humbly endured and borne the pangs of love, waiting for your good will; but I have in all cases found it harsh and wounding. And, since I am wholly at your command, I wonder greatly how your kindness can refuse me its favour when weeping and sighing I have begged for your mercy. Harder than a diamond, &c.

Alas! my lady, you have given me no comfort in my grief, no, none at all. Rather you have much discomfited me, so that I hate all discomfort. Yet nonetheless, I will henceforth love more strongly than ever before, and when your cruelty — all too fierce against me — has slain and destroyed me, then my constancy will be manifest. Harder than a diamond, &c.)

In this virelai by Guillaume de Machaut (c. 1300-77), the poet says that his lady's hardness towards him is greater than that of a diamond, but declares that he will remain loyal to her. The text is taken (by permission) from *One Hundred Ballades, Rondeaux and Virelais from the late Middle Ages,* edited by Nigel Wilkins, Cambridge University Press, 1969, pp. 34-5. The first section of the poem is sung in Machaut's own setting on the cassette accompanying this book. The setting is printed in *One Hundred Ballades ...,* pp. 158-9.

The lines have seven and four syllables, and there are only two rhymes, [ãn] and [e] in each stanza. Machaut uses some Picard forms, such as *vo* as well as *vostre, arez* as well as *avré,* the first presumably for metrical convenience.

By this time (c. 1350) all the vowels followed by a nasal consonant would be nasalized, though the vowels *i* and *u* in *un, simple, humblement,* etc., would not yet have their modern pronunciation of [ɛ̃] and [œ̃] respectively. The sound of the *o* in words like *donné* might be [ɔ̃] or [ũ]. It is likely that *vostre* and *volenté* would have [u] rather than [ɔ].

Many consonants would have ceased to be pronounced, not only at the end of words (except in liaison) but within them. Thus the *r* of *douceur, merci,* and *nonpourquant,* and the first *s* of *jusques* would be silent; the *s* of words like *vostre* and *sousriant* had of course fallen from speech two centuries earlier.

Both the spelling and the rhyme in *navré: avré* (lines 16-17) show how the diphthong [ai] became [e] in verb-endings, so that the past participle *navré* can rhyme with the future tense *avré.*

8

'**Je ne suis plus telx que soloye.**' an anonymous rondeau
which was set to music by Dufay.

About 1430.

> Je ne suis plus telx que soloye,
> J'ay perdu tout solas et joye,
> Devenu suy viel et usé,
> Et m'ont les dames refusé
> Quant plus servir ne les povoye.
>
> Jonesse me fault et monnoye
> Desquels tres enblé je m'aydoye,
> Et pour ce tout presupposé,
> Je ne suis plus, &c.
>
> Helas, se revenir sçavoie   10
> En l'estat où premier j'estoye,
> Je feroye fort du rusé.
> Et se j'en estoye acusé,
> Savés vous que responderoye?
> Je ne suis plus, &c.

(I'm not the man I used to be. I've lost all my zest and joy,
and grown old and worn. And the ladies have rejected me, now that
I'm no use to them any more.

I've lost my youth and my cash, which both served me well on
the sly: and granted all that, I'm not the man I used to be.

Alas! if I knew how to return to my first state, I'd be more
cunning. And if I were blamed for it, do you know what I'd reply?
I'm not the man I used to be.)

The anonymous poet strikes a familiar note of rueful self-deprecation, but does not expect to be taken very seriously. The refrain is woven in with dexterity.

The text is from Paris, Bibliothèque Nationale, MS n.a. fr. 6771, f. 97. The musical setting by Dufay is printed, among other places, in *One Hundred Ballades, Rondeaux and Virelais from the late Middle Ages*, edited by Nigel Wilkins, Cambridge, 1969, pp. 174-5.

The poet uses eight-syllable lines, with two rhymes in [ɛə] and [e]. Many of the former (lines 1, 5, 7, 10, 11, 14) are verbs used in the first person singular of the imperfect and conditional; these forms were of course di-syllabic, as can be seen from the scansion of line 12. The modern French form with *-ois,* and later still *-ais,* was not fully established until the 17th century.

The text illustrates well the conservative, indeed archaizing nature of French spelling in the later Middle Ages. The *s* of *estat, estoye, responderoye, desquels,* was silent; the *l* of *telx* and *fault* is an etymological survival; and the *c* of *sçavoie* results from a common misapprehension that the French verb derived from the Latin *scire.*

If one wishes to present this as a popular poem, the *r* of *perdu, servir* (both times), *pour* and *revenir* (final), and the *s* of *plus* and *helas,* will be silent.

9

'Avez point veu la Perronnelle,' a strophic song whose words and music are both anonymous.

About 1490.

Avez point veu la Perronnelle
Que les gendarmes ont amenée?

Ilz l'ont abillée comme ung paige:
C'est pour passer le Dauphiné.

Elle avoit troys mignons de freres,
Qui la sont allez pourchasser.

Tant l'ont cherchée que l'ont trouvée
A la fontaine d'un ver pré.

'Et Dieu vous gard, la Perronnelle!
Vous en voulez point retourner?'   10

'Et nenny vraiement, mes beaulx freres:
Jamés en France n'entreray.

Recommandez moy à mon pere,
Et à ma mere s'il vous plaist. '

(Have you seen La Perronnelle, whom the soldiers took away? They dressed her in page's clothes to go through Dauphiné. She had three fine brothers who went chasing after her. They searched so long that they found her, in a green meadow by a spring. 'God save you, Perronnelle! won't you come home?' 'Why, no indeed, good brothers, I'll never go back to France. Give good day to my father for me, and my mother too, if you please.')

This famous popular song survived until the 19th century, when it was collected orally in Piedmont and Catalonia. The present version is taken from Paris, Bibliothèque Nationale, MS fr. 12744, f. 27 verso, which also contains an anonymous musical setting for unaccompanied solo voice. The edition from this MS by G. Paris in *Chansons du XVᵉ Siècle*, Paris, 1875, is unreliable. The music is sung on the cassette accompanying this book. Another longer version of the poem, without music, is in *Chanson Verse of the Early Renaissance*, edited by Brian Jeffery, London, 1971, pp. 144-5.

Because of the popular style, many consonants can be assumed to be silent, like the *r* in *gendarmes, pour, pourchasser*, etc.; *ilz* in line 3 and *il* in line 14 would both be reduced to [i]. The spelling *ver pré* shows the *t* of *vert* to have dropped from speech. The *au* of *Dauphiné* would be [o] and *beaulx* would be [bəo]. The first vowel in *freres, pere, mere*, would be [e], not [ɛ] as now. Possibly the modern [wa] could be used in *troys, moy*, though [wɛ] is more likely.

10

'**Nous sommes de l'ordre de Saint Babouin,**' a strophic song whose words are anonymous and which was set to music by Compère.

About 1500.

Nous sommes de l'ordre
De Saint Babouin.
L'ordre ne dit mye
De lever matin;
Dormir jusque à prime!
Et boyre bon vin!
    Et din din din,
Et dire matines
Sur ung pot de vin!

A nostre disner   10
Le beau chapon gras,
La souppe au jaunet
Comme au mardi gras,
La piece de beuf
Et le gras mouton,
    Et don don don,
Et voylà la vie
Que nous demandon.

A nostre gouster
Le beau vin claret,   20
La belle salade
Au harenc soret,
Pastes de pigons
Si sont en saison,
    Et don don don,
Et velà la vie
Que nous demandon.

A nostre souper
Les connys rotis,
Faisans et butors   30
Et aussi perdrix,
Poussins à l'eaue rose
Et force chapons,
    Et don don don,
Et velà la vie
Que nous demandon.

Et apres souper
Le beau ypocras,
La tarte succrée
Au formaige gras,   40
Les poires confites
En plusieurs façons,
    Et don don don,
Et voylà la vie
Que nous demandon.

A nostre coucher
Nous aurons blans draps,
Et la belle fille
Entre nos deux bras,
Les tetins poignans,   50
La mote du con,
    Et don don don,
Et voylà la vie
Que nous demandon.

Et quant ce vint à l'eure
Que on sonne mynuit,
La fille s'esveille
Pour prendre deduit;
Le compaignon sault,
Chassant à son con,   60
    Et don don don,
Et voylà la vie
Que nous demandon.

A nostre lever
Les beaulx instrumens,
Trompetes et clarons,
Tabourins d'argent,
Enfans sans soucy
Jouans du bedon,
    Et don don don,   70
Et voylà la vie
Que nous demandon.

(We belong to the Order of St. Babouin. The Order doesn't tell us to get up early: let's sleep till prime, and drink good wine! Ding, dong, and say matins over a pot of wine!

A fine fat capon for lunch, egg soup as on Shrove Tuesday, a piece of beef and fat mutton — ding, dong, and that's the life for us.

Fine claret wine to sip, a good salad of pickled herring, pigeon pie when it's in season — ding, dong, and that's the life for us.

Roast rabbits for supper, pheasants, bitterns and partridges, chickens cooked in rose water and plenty of capons — ding, dong, and that's the life for us.

And after supper good spiced wine, a sweet tart with rich cheese, preserved pears of all sorts — ding, dong, and that's the life for us.

We'll have white sheets for our bed, and a beautiful girl in our arms, her rising breasts and the mound of her cunt — ding, dong, and that's the life for us.

And when midnight sounds, the girl wakes up for her sport; we'll leap up, and hunt for her cunt — ding, dong, and that's the life for us.

Fine instruments when we get up, trumpets and bugles, silver drums, the Enfans sans Soucy playing on their drum — ding, dong, and that's the life for us.)

This poem in praise of wine and good living is taken from a collection of chanson verse printed in about 1520, edited by Brian Jeffery in *Chanson Verse of the Early Renaissance,* London, 1971, pp. 123-6. A musical setting (unfortunately without words) by Loyset Compère was printed in 1501, showing that the poem existed at least as early as that, though not necessarily in exactly the same form as the present version.

The musical setting by Compère is recorded on the cassette accompanying this book. The music is printed in Compère's *Opera Omnia,* edited by Ludwig Finscher, vol. V (American Institute of Musicology, 1972), pp. 41-2, but without the words, which have been specially underlaid for this cassette by Brian Jeffery.

Like 'Avez point veu la Perronnelle', this song survived through the centuries. Georges Delarue remembers singing it as a student in Paris in 1946, under the title 'Nous sommes les moines de Saint Bernardin' ('Chansons folkloriques de la Renaissance', *Le Monde Alpin et Rhodanien, Revue Régionale d'Ethnologie,* 2, 1973, pp. 61-4).

The content of the poem has behind it a long if not entirely respectable tradition. There is the obvious mockery of monastic asceticism with its rule of poverty, chastity and obedience, and the substitution for them of a 'pot de vin' and a 'belle fille', lickerishly described. But the hankering after comfort and luxury is something more than a joke. For centuries men lived on a mainly subsistence economy, with limited resources, inadequate storage and preservation of food and fuel, and few imported goods to make them independent of local and seasonal products. Sweetstuffs, for example, were a prized treat; salt beef and hard tack, straw and sacking, were the general lot. Poems like this, and there are many such, with their yearning for enriched soups, plump game, sweets and clean linen show us the truly inaccessible dreams of the common man.

The language of the poem, like 'Avez point veu la Perronelle', reflects 'popular' French. The spelling of the refrain in stanzas 3 and 4 shows how the *oi* or *oy* of *voilà* was simplified to [ɛ], though one might well hear the modern French [wa] in words like *boyre, poires.* Additional popular features would be the modern French [ɛ̃] in words like *vin, matin,* where 'correct' French would be [ĩ], and perhaps [ũ] not [ɔ̃] in *mouton, saison,* and the ring of bells chorus *don don don.*

These two poems should be compared with nos. 11 (du Bellay) and 12 (Ronsard) to show the variables in language development. The concept of 'registers' appropriate to differing social, literary or personal contexts is today accepted for our contemporary language; it is equally essential for an understanding of the past. The criterion of suitability to context is more useful than dichotomies between conservative and innovatory, slovenly and pedantic, prescriptive and permissive tendencies which so often prejudge the issue.

11

'**La nuyt froyde et sombre**,' two stanzas of an ode by du
Bellay, which were set to music by Lassus.

1549.

> La nuyt froyde et sombre
> Couvrant d'obscure umbre
> La terre et les cieux,
> Aussi doulx que miel
> Fait couler du ciel
> Le someil aux yeux.
>
> Puis le jour luysant
> Au labeur duysant
> Sa lueur expose,
> Et d'un teint divers   10
> Ce grand univers
> Tapisse et compose.

(The chill dark night, spreading its black shade over land and
heaven, brings slumber flowing sweet as honey to our eyes.

Then gleaming day, guiding us to toil, shows forth its light, and
weaves with varied hue the pattern of this mighty universe.)

These two descriptive stanzas are taken from du Bellay's
ode *De l'inconstance des choses,* 1549; modern edition in
his *Œuvres Poétiques,* ed. H. Chamard, III, Paris, 1912,
pp. 15-21. The music is sung on the cassette accompanying
this book, and is published, among other places, in Lassus'
Madrigale & Chansons, ed. H. Besseler, *Das Chorwerk,* 13,
1931. Lassus set only these two stanzas, and he deliberately
makes all four voices come together, for the only time in the
piece, on the first syllable of *univers.* In line 7, *luysant* is
the original reading, not *suivant.*

This poem and the following one by Ronsard may be
considered together, for linguistic purposes, as examples of

'correct' French of the 16th century. Thus the sound in words like *un* might still be [ỹ], although in less formal contexts it would be the modern [œ̃]; the sound in *sombre, combat,* etc., would be [ɔ̃] not [ũ]; and the *oi* or *oy* of *froyde, boit,* etc., would be [wɛ]. The nasal consonants would be pronounced as well as the nasal vowels, but many final consonants would be silent except where required for liaison. Thus in no. 11, *labeur* in line 8 would have a silent *r*, but in the following line *lueur* would sound the *r* before *expose*. In no. 12, the *t* of *ront* is twice pronounced in line 4 but the *t* of *boit* is silent in line 11, as is the *r* of *languir* in line 13. As Ronsard's poem is built on antithetical phrases, however, there are many rhetorical pauses, for example after the fourth syllable of lines 2, 3, 4, 8, where a final consonant would be sounded even though liaison is not involved. The loss of final *l* is shown by the rhyme *seuls: paresseus* (lines 12-13). Other points to note are: *obscure* would not sound the *b*; *expose* would be pronounced with [s], not [ks]; *presque* would have a silent *s*; the vowel in the feminine indefinite article *une* would no longer be nasalized; *someil* would still have [ʎ], not [j]; *eau* would be [əo], not [o].

12

'**Amour et Mars sont presque d'une sorte**', a sonnet by Ronsard.

1560.

> Amour et Mars sont presque d'une sorte:
> L'un en plain jour, l'autre combat de nuit,
> L'un aus rivaus, l'autre aus gensdarmes nuit,
> L'un ront un huis, l'autre ront une porte.
>
> L'un finement trompe une vile forte,
> L'autre coiment une maison seduit:
> L'un un butin, l'autre le gain poursuit,
> L'un deshonneur, l'autre dommage aporte.
>
> L'un couche à terre, et l'autre gist souvent
> Devant un huis à la froideur du vent: 10
> L'un boit meinte eau, l'autre boit meinte larme.
>
> Mars va tout seul, les Amours vont tout seuls:
> Qui voudra donc ne languir paresseus,
> Soit l'un ou l'autre, amoureus ou gendarme.

(Cupid and Mars are almost of a kind. One fights by broad daylight, the other by night. One wounds his rivals, the other his foes; one storms a lady's door, the other a city's gate; one cleverly takes a fortress by guile, the other slyly cajoles a house into surrender; one chases booty, the other pursues his gain; one brings dishonour, the other distress; one sleeps rough on the ground, the other many a night in the bitter wind outside a door; often the one swallows water, the other his tears. Mars walks alone, and so does love. So, let him who chooses not to pine in idleness be one or the other — lover or warrior.)

Ronsard compares the god of love to the god of war. Phrase after phrase in his poem shows in what ways they are similar; phrase after phrase, in what ways they are different.

The text is from Ronsard's *Œuvres,* 1560 (British Museum copy). This sonnet was first published in Ronsard's *Amours* in 1552, but altered in minor details for the 1560 and later editions. Guillaume Boni set it to music, and as it was the 1560 version that he set, we have adopted that version here. Boni's setting is published in *Anthologie de la Chanson Parisienne au XVIe Siècle,* edited by François Lesure, Monaco, 1953, no. 34. For linguistic notes, see no. 11 above.